Say It, Sign It

Written by Elaine Epstein

Illustrated by Mary O'Keefe Young

SCHOLASTIC INC.

New York   Toronto   London   Auckland   Sydney

D1730610

For Sonya Sofranko

Copyright © 1994 by Scholastic Inc.
All rights reserved. Published by Scholastic Inc.
Printed in the U.S.A.
ISBN 0-590-27387-6

45 44 43 42 41 40 39 38   08   9 10 11 12 / 0

Todd and Sonya ran to the water.
A wave rushed up to them and
water tickled their toes.

3

They told each other about the sea.
Todd said the word *waves*. Sonya
signed the word *water*.

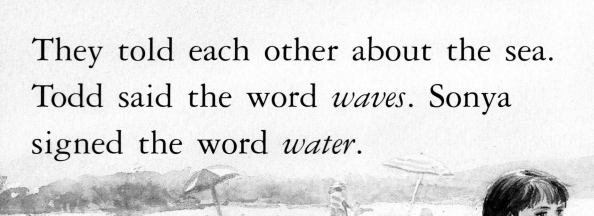

water

5

Sonya and Todd sat on the wet sand
and looked out at the sea.
"Wow! Look!" said Todd.
"Pretty boat," signed Sonya.

pretty   boat

7

Then they used shovels and rakes
to make the sand into shapes.
"Great snake!" signed Sonya.
"Nice castle," Todd said.

great

snake

9

A man in a funny bathing suit
came along. Sonya signed, "Grandpa!"
Todd said and signed, "Grandpa!"

Grandpa

11

Grandpa worked hard in the sand.
He dug and shoveled and raked.
Lumps and bumps of sand flew
everywhere!

my · car

Todd and Sonya
sat in the holes.
"My car!" said Todd.
"My car!" signed Sonya.

Later, a woman in a yellow sun hat
came along.

"Grandma!" signed Sonya.

"Grandma!" said Todd.

Grandma

15

Together,
they told Grandma
the story of their day.

fun

Todd said it.
Sonya signed it.